A STUDIO PRESS BOOK

First published in the UK in 2023 by Studio Press,
an imprint of Bonnier Books UK,
4th Floor, Victoria House, Bloomsbury Square, London WC1B 4DA
Owned by Bonnier Books,
Sveavägen 56, Stockholm, Sweden

www.bonnierbooks.co.uk

Printed in China
3 5 7 9 10 8 6 4

All rights reserved
ISBN 978-1-80078-676-9

Written by Nate Rae
Edited by Frankie Jones
Designed by Maddox Philpot
Illustrated by Adam Doyle, Junis Laureano and Marcos Keller
Production by Giulia Caparrelli

WHO'S THAT, SWINGING FROM BUILDING TO BUILDING ACROSS NEW YORK? IT'S SPIDER-MAN... IN FACT, IT'S A WHOLE ARRAY OF SPIDER-HEROES! THE MULTIVERSE IS MYSTERIOUSLY OPENING UP AS MORE AND MORE UNIVERSES COLLIDE, AND THE RESULT IS A WHOLE HOST OF NEW SUPER HEROES. KEEP AN EYE OUT FOR SPIDER-MAN AND HIS BUDDIES AS YOU EXPLORE THIS BOOK AND UNCOVER WHY THESE MULTI-DIMENSIONAL PORTALS ARE OPENING.

SPIDER-MAN (MILES MORALES)

ORIGINALLY FROM AN ALTERNATE UNIVERSE, MILES WAS BITTEN BY A GENETICALLY ENGINEERED SPIDER, GIVING HIM EXTRA SPIDER-POWERS, LIKE INVISIBILITY.

SPIDER-MAN (PETER PARKER)

AFTER BEING BITTEN BY A RADIOACTIVE SPIDER, PETER GAINED SPIDER-LIKE POWERS. NOW, HE PROTECTS THE STREETS OF NEW YORK AS WEB-SLINGING SUPER HERO SPIDER-MAN.

SPIDER-HAM (PETER PORKER)

SPIDER-HAM WAS BORN A SPIDER, AND GAINED HIS CURRENT FORM AFTER BEING BITTEN BY A RADIOACTIVE PIG.

ARAÑA (ANYA CORAZON)

AFTER NEARLY DYING, ANYA'S LIFE WAS SAVED WHEN A MAGE GAVE HER A SPIDER-SHAPED TATTOO. SHE GAINED SPIDER-POWERS IN THE PROCESS.

SP//DR

PENI PARKER IS RARELY SEEN WITHOUT HER ENORMOUS ROBOTIC SP//DR SUIT, WHICH CONTAINS A FRIEND OF HERS – THE RADIOACTIVE SPIDER WHO BIT HER.

GHOST-SPIDER (GWEN STACEY)

WHEN SHE'S NOT GOING TO HIGH SCHOOL OR DRUMMING IN HER BAND, THE MARY JANES, GWEN STACY FIGHTS CRIME AS THE HOODIE-WEARING GHOST-SPIDER.

SPIDER-MAN NOIR

BY DAY, THIS BROODING VERSION OF PETER PARKER IS AN INVESTIGATIVE JOURNALIST. BY NIGHT, HE PARKOURS ACROSS THE NEW YORK SKYLINE, TAKING ON CRIMINALS.

SILK

CINDY MOON GOT HER POWERS FROM THE SAME SPIDER THAT BIT PETER PARKER, GIVING HER THE ABILITY TO TRACK SPIDER-MAN ANYWHERE IN THE MULTIVERSE.

WELCOME TO THE MULTIVERSE!

SOMETHING VERY STRANGE IS HAPPENING ACROSS THE MULTIVERSE – MORE AND MORE PORTALS ARE POPPING UP ALL ACROSS NEW YORK AS UNIVERSES COLLIDE. LUCKILY, EACH UNIVERSE COMES WITH ITS OWN FRIENDLY NEIGHBOURHOOD SPIDER-HERO, READY TO JOIN FORCES AND INVESTIGATE THE WEIRD GOINGS-ON.

CHAOS IN QUEENS

A CLASS ACT

PIG IN THE CITY

THE DOCTOR IS IN

DOWN IN THE LAB

BACK IN TIME

ALL ABOARD!

DON'T RAIN ON THE PARADE

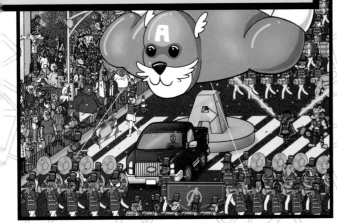

UN-CONVENTIONAL

THE WORLDS COLLIDE

AFTER DARK

COLLEGE DAYS

HITTING THE ROOF

A DAY AT THE PARK

CHAOS IN QUEENS

SOMETHING STRANGE IS HAPPENING IN QUEENS! A PORTAL HAS OPENED UP AND SPIDER-HEROES FROM ACROSS THE MULTIVERSE ARE STARTING TO POP UP ALL ACROSS NEW YORK. LOOK OUT FOR PETER PARKER, MILES MORALES, SPIDER-HAM, GHOST-SPIDER, SP//DR, SPIDER-MAN NOIR, ARAÑA AND SILK.

A CLASS ACT

IT'S NOT EASY BALANCING BEING A FRIENDLY NEIGHBOURHOOD SUPER HERO AND GOING TO HIGH SCHOOL EVERY DAY, PARTICULARLY WHEN MORE AND MORE WEIRD PORTALS ARE POPPING UP IN CLASS! KEEP AN EYE OUT FOR MILES MORALES AND HIS FELLOW SPIDER-HEROES AS THEY INVESTIGATE.

PIG IN THE CITY

DON'T LET THE HUMANS HOG ALL THE ATTENTION! IN BETWEEN STOPPING PIGGY-BANK ROBBERS IN THEIR TRACKS, SPIDER-HAM HAS BEEN LOOKING INTO THE EMERGENCE OF PORTALS IN OTHER WORLDS, TOO – SPECIFICALLY HIS OWN WORLD, EARTH-8311'S NEW YORK, NEW YOLK CITY.

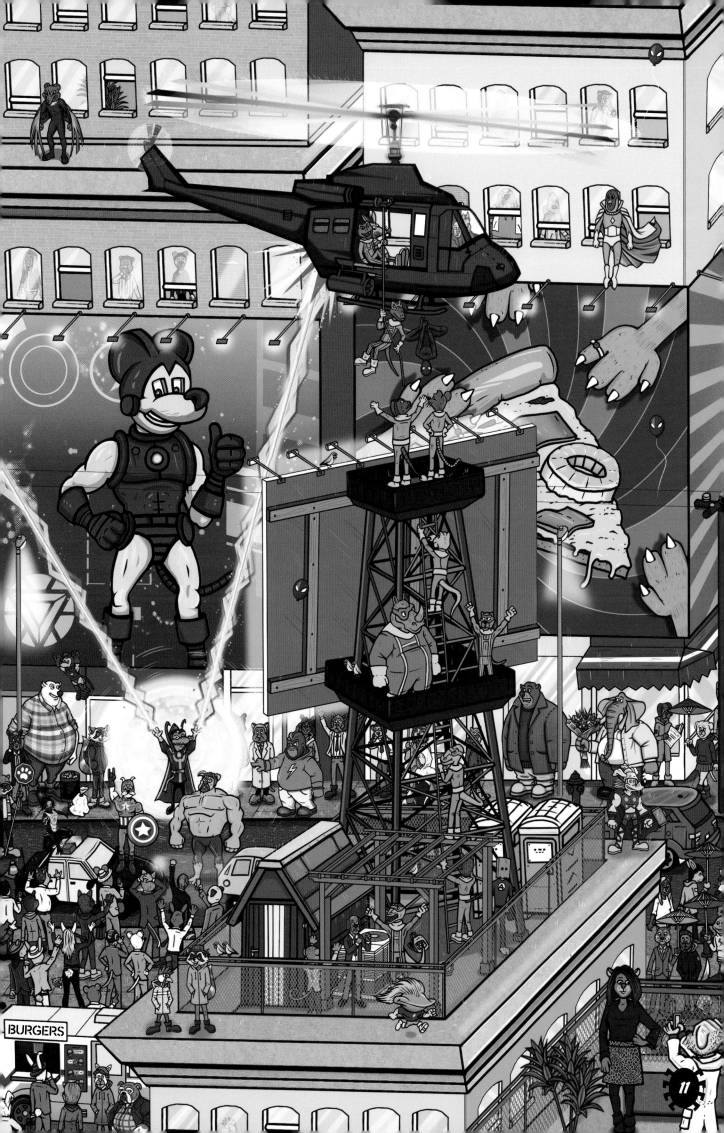

BURGERS

THE DOCTOR IS IN

WHEN SOMETHING STRANGE IS GOING ON, WHO BETTER TO GO TO THAN NEW YORK'S RESIDENT SORCERER, DOCTOR STRANGE? A FEW BOOKS AND A SHORT INVESTIGATION LATER, THE DOCTOR IS CERTAIN THAT SOME STOLEN TECH IS RESPONSIBLE FOR THE MYSTERIOUS PORTALS. LOOK FOR SPIDER-MAN OUTSIDE THE DOCTOR'S BASE, THE SANCTUM SANTORUM.

DOWN IN THE LAB

THERE'S ONE SPIDER-HERO WHO KNOWS MORE ABOUT TECH THAN ALMOST ANYBODY ELSE, AND THAT'S PENI PARKER, EXPERT PILOT OF THE MECHANICAL SP//DR SUIT. WHILE SHE LOOKS INTO THE STOLEN EQUIPMENT, TRY TO SPOT THE REST OF THE GANG EXPLORING HER LAB.

BACK IN TIME

THINGS ARE LOOKING EVEN GRIMMER THAN NORMAL IN 1930s NEW YORK. CLAD IN HIS EXPLOSION-PROOF SUIT, SPIDER-MAN NOIR IS HOT ON THE TAIL OF CRIMINALS FROM ALL OVER THE MULTIVERSE, SET ON CAUSING CHAOS IN HIS CITY. BUT WHICH ONE OF THEM IS RESPONSIBLE FOR ALL THOSE PORTALS?

ISLAND FERRY

AFTER DARK

IT'S NIGHT-TIME IN NEW YORK AND MANY OF QUEENS' RESIDENTS ARE SAFELY INDOORS – BUT THAT DOESN'T MEAN SPIDER-MAN GETS A NIGHT OFF! MILES AND HIS FRIENDS ARE NOW CERTAIN THEY KNOW WHO THEIR VILLAIN IS: DOCTOR OCTOPUS, WHO'S BEEN OPENING PORTALS ALL OVER THE MULTIVERSE IN ORDER TO CREATE A SINISTER SIX... ENTIRELY MADE UP OF DOC OCKS! NOW TO TRACK HIM DOWN...

COLLEGE DAYS

WITH THE DOC OCK VARIANTS DEALT WITH, IT'S UP TO THE TEAM TO LOCATE ALL THE STOLEN TECH BEFORE THE MULTIVERSE CAN OPEN ANY FURTHER AND CAUSE MORE CHAOS. LET'S START WHERE IT ALL BEGAN – EMPIRE STATE UNIVERSITY, WHERE PETER PARKER WAS FIRST BITTEN BY A RADIOACTIVE SPIDER... AND DOC OCK'S OLD WORKPLACE.

SCIENCE FAIR

UN-CONVENTIONAL

ON THE HUNT FOR THE REST OF THE STOLEN EQUIPMENT, SPIDER-HERO ARAÑA KNOWS JUST WHERE TO FIND THE BIGGEST GATHERING OF SUPER HERO EXPERTS IN TOWN – A LOCAL CONVENTION. AS AN ADDED BONUS, OUR HEROES CAN BLEND INTO THE CROWD TO AVOID BEING RECOGNISED.

THINGS HULK SMASHED!

ARCHIVE

HITTING THE ROOF

SILK AND THE REST OF THE TEAM ARE GATHERING THE LAST OF THE STOLEN TECH, READY TO RETURN IT TO ITS RIGHTFUL HOME. BUT WHAT'S THAT LOOMING IN THE SKY ABOVE NEW YORK CITY? OUR HEROES WILL NEED TO WORK FAST IF THEY'RE GOING TO STOP THE MULTIVERSE COLLIDING WITH ITSELF.

THE WORLDS COLLIDE

THINGS ARE WEIRDER THAN EVER, AS WORLDS FROM ALL OVER THE MULTIVERSE LEAK INTO EACH OTHER. ONLY THE SPIDER-SQUAD CAN HELP, USING THE TECH THEY'VE GATHERED TO CLOSE THE PORTALS FOR GOOD... BEFORE IT'S TOO LATE.

A DAY AT THE PARK

WITH THE MYSTERY SOLVED AND DOC OCK DEFEATED, IT'S FINALLY TIME FOR THE SPIDER-TEAM TO RELAX! JOIN GHOST-SPIDER AND HER FRIENDS AS THEY ENJOY A DAY IN THE PARK BEFORE RETURNING TO THEIR OWN WORLDS.

MORE CHARACTERS AND OBJECTS TO SEARCH AND FIND

CHAOS IN QUEENS

- LOST YELLOW HAT
- CAPTAIN AMERICA'S SHIELD
- SPIDER-MAN STREET ART
- UNION JACK MOTORCYCLE HELMET
- SPOT
- GAMBIT
- YELLOW CAB
- NICK FURY

A CLASS ACT

- GANKE LEE
- AMERICAN FOOTBALL
- BASKETBALL
- FLOWER HAIRCLIP
- LOVE LETTER
- SUNGLASSES
- SPIDEY BALLOONS
- DROPPED BOOKS

PIG IN THE CITY

- DOCTOR OCTOPUSSYCAT
- IRONMOUSE
- FREE HUGS SIGN
- FOOD DELIVERY BIKE
- RAVEN THE HUNTER
- BAG-MAN
- BUNCH OF FLOWERS
- THRR

THE DOCTOR IS IN

- DOCTOR STRANGE
- BEAST
- A DRONE
- INFINITY GAUNTLET
- OSCORP BOX
- BLACK CAT
- PINK DOUGHNUT
- COLOSSUS

DOWN IN THE LAB

- M.O.D.O.K.
- RED BOOK
- SP//DR SCHEMATICS
- GREEN HARD HAT
- MYSTERIO
- KEYBOARD
- SPIDER-MAN PLUSHIE
- BLUE CLIPBOARD

BACK IN TIME

- MORBIUS
- CAKE WITH PINK ICING
- JUGGERNAUT
- LOKI
- PAIR OF GLOVES
- KINGPIN
- HOWARD STARK
- THE SHOCKER

ALL ABOARD!

- SPIDER-PUNK
- AMERICAN FLAG
- OSCORP BOX
- BANANA SKIN
- THE LIZARD
- MISSING DOG POSTER
- BEACH BALL
- SABRETOOTH

AFTER DARK

- UNION JACK GUITAR
- SACK OF MONEY
- CAPTAIN MARVEL
- WOLVERINE
- SPIDER-MAN: INDIA
- MIDTOWN HIGH SCHOOL LETTERMAN JACKET
- FIRE HYDRANT
- PAINTER / DECORATOR

DON'T RAIN ON THE PARADE

- CROCTOR STRANGE
- PORK GRIND
- PURPLE PARASOL
- HOBGOBBLER
- SCARLET POOCH AND PIGEON
- NEWS REPORTER
- GIRAFFE SPECTATOR
- BUZZARD

COLLEGE DAYS

- CHARLES XAVIER
- FRISBEE
- GUITAR
- ORANGE MOPED
- CYCLE HELMET
- FAN MEETING CAPTAIN AMERICA
- SAUSAGE DOG
- ANGEL

UN-CONVENTIONAL

- ARTIST
- VULTURE
- QUICKSILVER
- CHILD'S IRON MAN COSPLAY
- CRACKED CAPTAIN AMERICA SHIELD
- HULK COSPLAY
- INFLATABLE TUBE SPIDER-MAN
- VISION

HITTING THE ROOF

- SELFIE STICK
- SILVER SURFER
- RED AND WHITE BASEBALL CAP
- CAT IN RUCKSACK
- CYCLOPS
- SPIDER-MAN T-SHIRT
- QUICKSILVER
- JJ JAMESON

THE WORLDS COLLIDE

- WASP
- WATERCOOLER
- HUMAN TORCH
- DORMAMMU
- LADY OCTOPUS
- TAKEAWAY NOODLES
- STORM
- SPIDER-MAN 2099

A DAY AT THE PARK

- COUPLE GETTING ENGAGED
- BASEBALL BAT
- SKATEBOARD
- BANSHEE
- SURFING DOG
- BLACK PANTHER
- SLICE OF PIZZA
- MR FANTASTIC

ANSWERS

PETER PARKER, MILES MORALES, SPIDER-HAM, SP//DR, SPIDER-MAN NOIR, ARAÑA, GHOST-SPIDER, AND SILK ARE CIRCLED IN YELLOW, AND THE OTHER CHARACTERS AND OBJECTS TO SEARCH AND FIND ARE CIRCLED IN BLUE.

CHAOS IN QUEENS

A CLASS ACT

PIG IN THE CITY

THE DOCTOR IS IN

DOWN IN THE LAB

BACK IN TIME

ALL ABOARD!

AFTER DARK

DON'T RAIN ON THE PARADE

COLLEGE DAYS

UN-CONVENTIONAL

HITTING THE ROOF

THE WORLDS COLLIDE

A DAY AT THE PARK